Thoughts on religi

C000051794

N. S. Talbot

Alpha Editions

This edition published in 2023

ISBN : 9789357944588

Design and Setting By
Alpha Editions
www.alphaedis.com
Email - info@alphaedis.com

Contents

PREFACE

I send out this little and fragmentary book with the consciousness that it calls for apology. I have had to write it hastily during a short period of leave. Yet it touches upon great subjects which deserve the reverence of leisurely writing. Ought I not, then, to have waited for the leisure of days after the war? I think not. Such days may never come. And, in any case, *now* is the time for the Church to think intently about the war and its issues, and to learn from them. The Church is far more than a department of 'the services,' the resources of which it is[Pg vi] convenient to mobilise as so much more munition of war. She is the perpetual protagonist in the world of the Kingdom of God. War for her, if for nobody else, should be an apocalypse, that is, a vision of realities for which at all times she is bound to fight, of which, nevertheless, she is apt to lose sight during the engrossments of peace. It is as lit up by the cruel light of war's conflagrations that the things concerning the Kingdom must be seized anew. If anybody has thoughts which he feels he must share with others, he should not postpone doing so. He should communicate his thoughts to others in order that he may learn from their comments and criticism. I can claim, whilst asking pardon for whatever may offend in them, that the thoughts represented by the following pages have[Pg vii] not been come by hastily, but have been growing in my mind during the long months at the front since the beginning of the war. They have, so to say, been hammered out as metal upon the anvil of war.

They are thoughts about religion. Nothing is so important as religion; nothing is more potent than true ideas in religion. Deep fountains of real religion—of simple and unself-prizing faith—have been unsealed by the convulsion of war. Yet this religion is weak in ideas, and some of the ideas with which it is bound up are wrong ideas. Men of our race are very sure that it matters more what a man is than what he thinks. British religion is deep and rich, but it is, characteristically, deeper and richer in what it is than in what it knows itself to be.[Pg viii] It sorely needs a mind of strong and compelling conviction. If these pages were to help ever so few readers towards being possessed anew of the truth of the Gospel of God in Christ, their appearance would be justified.

I have written, perhaps, as one who dreads saying 'Peace, where there is no peace.' I would rather err on the side of emphasising criticism and difficulty than the other way. There is, indeed, little room for complacency in a Christian, still less in an English Churchman, at the front. Yet in 'padres' hope and expectation should predominate, and these as based less upon results achieved than upon the mutual understanding, respect, and indeed affection which increasingly unite them to the men whom they would serve.

And in them, too, if[Pg ix] they are 'C. of E.,' there should be growing, along with an unevasive discontent, a sanguine loyalty to their mother Church. For all that she now means so little to so many she will yet win a more than nominal allegiance from many of her wandering children. For there is in her, beneath the surface of her sluggish confusion, a living heart and candid mind, upon which is being written afresh the good news in Christ. She is being vivified, as perhaps no other part of Christendom, into readiness for the future.

N.S.T.

B.E.F., *November 1916.*

'And the loftiness of man shall be bowed down, and the haughtiness of men shall be brought low: and the Lord alone shall be exalted in that day. And the idols shall utterly pass away. And men shall go into the caves of the rocks, and into the holes of the earth, from before the terror of the Lord and from the glory of His majesty, when He ariseth to shake mightily the earth.'

'Whom ye ignorantly worship, Him declare I unto you.'

I

I write this little book in order to help towards an answer to the question, How is it with the Christian religion at the front? With the flower of British manhood massed in the Army this and like questions are bound to arise— How is it with the men? Where are they religiously? What do they want? What will they need when they return? and so forth. There never has been such an opportunity of taking a comparative view of British Christianity and of framing answers to such questions. Perhaps those who are working as chaplains at the front are especially challenged to attempt these tasks. Their answer must not be loose or sentimental. There is a danger of that. The emotions aroused by the war may encourage sentimental verdicts. That may be the reason why a good many ideas which are current at home about religion at the front, are a good distance removed from reality.

II

I can only venture upon a verdict after first acknowledging that it is inseparably bound up with my own shortcomings. Other men of a truer devotion and love may well have grounds in a more effective ministry for challenging and amplifying it.

Further, I have to ask that allowance be made for the fact that men like myself, who have been working as 'C. of E.' chaplains, are not very well qualified to speak about the religion of the men. There is something wrong about the status of chaplains. They belong to what the author of *A Student in Arms* calls 'the super-world' of officers, which as such is separate from the men. As a class we find it hard to penetrate the surface of the men—that surface which we can almost see thrust out at us like a shield, in the suddenly assumed rigidity of men as they salute us. We are in an unchristian position, in the sense that we are in a position which Christ would not have occupied. He, I am sure, would have been a regimental stretcher-bearer, truly among and of the men. We are very unlike Him. We are often liked, and are thought good fellows, but we are unlike Him and miss what He could discover. Our—my—verdict is not necessarily His.

Lastly, all verdicts must be rough in war. The nature of war and of its effects often precludes any one from knowing exactly what is going on in the souls of men. War is a muddy business, encasing the body in dirt, and caking over the soul. It forms hard surfaces over the centres of sensitiveness. It is benumbing to spiritual faculties. That is nature's way of accommodation with war's environment. To feel things much would literally be maddening. To brood about danger, to apprehend or anticipate or philosophise may imperil 'nerve.' Rather the majority of men carry on, callously, almost gaily, with mental and spiritual faculties if possible inactive. I have met an entirely devout lover of music (since killed in action) who told me that he didn't miss music out here because "he wasn't carrying on with those faculties." I have seen a man of indubitable Christian conviction come down from the cold clam of the trenches in mid-winter and take up a religious book which ordinarily would have excited him and say—"Ah! yes, there is all that." I could almost see the surface which war had hardened over him. Beneath it in him and all the rest, who knows what may not be in process, ready to emerge when they can bathe in the solvent waters of peace?

Meanwhile they 'carry on.' That I think is especially congenial to the British. There is no doubt that men of our race have an invincibility, which is due in part to the fact that they do not think about or feel what is really going on. To be practically and sensually occupied with the passing moment is the way to carry on in war. It is characteristic of our men. They are remarkably void of apprehension in every sense of the word. Had the rank and file who fought the first battle of Ypres—when the whole of the British forces came to be strung out from Ypres to La Bassée in one line without a reserve—formed a general apprehension of and as to their position, they would have been 'rattled' and broken. They were not beaten, in part because they did not think of being beaten. "You can't," as they sing, "beat the boys of the bull-dog breed," but this invincibility has not altogether the virtue of facts understood, faced, and triumphed over. In short, British qualities and defects of qualities are closely interwoven. But my point is, that this being so, any verdict about what is going on in British souls during a war must be humble and tentative and patient of qualification.

III

On the whole, I venture to say, there is not a great revival of the Christian religion at the front. Yet I am eager to acclaim the wonderful quality of spirit which men of our race display in this war, and to claim it as Christian and God-inspired. Deep in their hearts is a great trust and faith in God. It is an inarticulate faith expressed in deeds. The top levels, as it were, of their consciousness, are much filled with grumbling and foul language and physical occupations; but beneath lie deep spiritual springs, whence issue their cheerfulness, stubbornness, patience, generosity, humility, and willingness to suffer and to die. They declare by what they are and do that there is a worthwhileness in effort and sacrifice. Without saying so, they commit themselves to "the Everlasting Arms."

The metaphor of human nature being hardened or caked over by war must be modified so as to allow that war lays human nature bare. It is a grand fibre or grain of British nature which the war has exposed. It is inwrought with Christian excellences of humility, unselfishness, fortitude, and all that makes a good comrade. It is precious stuff. Let there be no talk hereafter of the decadence of the race. Let no one dare to disparage the masses of our people; nor let any one, through class ignorance or prejudice or fear, speak of them contemptuously. They are priceless raw material. As I have hovered in seeming priestly impotence over miracles of cheerful patience lying on stretchers in dressing-stations, I have said—I have vowed to myself—"Here are men worth doing anything for."

There is a great heart in the people. It is not a great mind. In officers and men there is little intellectual grip upon what we are fighting for. Every one nearly is without a saving touch of rhetoric. Ideas are under suspicion. "Padre, what you say is just ideal, it's all in the air." But the objectors stick it and die for the unformulated and unexpressed ideal. They are far wiser and better than they know.

IV

I must modify, then, and say that on the whole there is not a great articulate revival of the Christian religion at the front. But further I must add that there is religion about, only, very often it is not the Christian religion. Rather it is natural religion. It is the expression of a craving for security. Literally it is a looking for salvation. It is a very unnatural man who does not feel at any rate more inclined to pray when danger abounds and anxiety presses, than at other times. Naturally, then, chaplains find a readier response to their efforts right at the front than farther back. Men come to a service before they go to the trenches. Communicants increase before a fight. Chaplains are frequently told of prayer being resorted to under this or that strain of this terrific war. There is in short a general association of ideas about religion and, as I have said, it may be called the association of a craving for security.

I would say nothing disrespectful of it. I would not pretend for a moment to be void of this very natural craving. I would recognise that impressions made by strain and anxiety are often the means whereby God brings men home to Himself. I thought it a hard saying of an ardent salvationist lad, who told me of a transport sergeant's prayers one night in a ditch by a shrapnelled roadside, and of the same sergeant's reversion to apparent irreligion on return to safety. "I call it," said the boy, "cowardice." But what I do say about it is, firstly, that religion thus mainly associated with danger, is not the Christian religion, and secondly, that many of the best men of all ranks have little to do with it, or what little they do have is intermittent and rather shamefaced.

I leave the first statement for the moment. About the second I hazard the belief that this has been more or less true of all soldiers in history. Religion regarded *merely* as a resort in trouble, as a possible source of good luck, as a charm or insurance policy is as old as man; but I believe many of the best soldiers up and down history have had little to do with it, and the more sporting and soldierly the man, the less he has had to do with it. After all, the soldier-man's code goes clean the other way. It is ever insisting on non-calculating and self-regardless service, endurance, and sacrifice. As such, it lies above the ordinary level of life, calling out the heroic and honourable in men. But religion associated with anxiety touches men at a level lower than the highest in them, it has the morbidity of their weaker moments hanging about it, it wears badly, and, above all, often it does not seem to work. I have had the case propounded to me of "Bill who did pray," but yet had had "his head blowed off."

V

I recur, then, to my verdict that on the whole there is not a great revival of the Christian religion at the front. Why is this?

First, war is war, and, what is more, this war is this war. I will not attempt to paint the picture. Every one must realise by now that the main concentration of all military effort is directed at creating in the trenches an ever-intenser inferno of heavy shells. In a great army there is every degree of risk to be run or immunity to be enjoyed; but at the very front, where all is stripped and laid bare, modern warfare is at times a furnace of horror. Its smoke darkens the heavens, thickening the "clouds and darkness" round about God, and deepening His silence. Its white heat scorches out human confidence in Him. He does not seem to count. There are stars in the darkness of war—stars which are the achievements of man's indomitable spirit. But God-ward there seems sometimes to be great darkness.

Further, war, despite all the easy things said in its praise, is a great iniquity. It is, as others have said, hell. As an environment to the soul it is, for all the countervailing heroisms of men, a world of evil power let loose.

And, again, war abounds in a number of trials—mostly associated with the extremes of heat and cold and damp and fatigue—for which, as the phrase goes, religion seems not to afford the slightest relief. It is a very physical business, squeezing out or overlaying the spiritual in men, though powerless wholly to extinguish it. War being what it is, the absence of religious revival during its course is not surprising. I have come to be very doubtful whether there is truth in the prevalent notion that war as such and automatically makes men better.

Secondly, that element in religion which can survive the weather of war must be a very hardy growth, something deeply engrained and habitual— something rock-built. And that is just what is lacking among men of our race. As an Anglican priest I reach here a glaring fact about the English Church. The war reveals that there are few men in its loose membership who are possessed by and instructed in its faith. Religion, as taught by the Church of England, has a feeble grip on the masses. They hold it in no familiar embrace. And if reasons are sought, they are partly found in the want of cutting edge to her sober comprehensive teaching, partly in the characteristics often theoretically so justifiable but practically so awkward, of the Prayer Book. There is little in our Church which corresponds to that elemental regimen or discipline which possesses simple-minded Roman Catholics. The power of cultus, of institutional and family religion, is largely absent.

To explain this brings me to a third reason why, under the stress of war, English Christianity is hardly in revival, namely, Bible difficulties. The Prayer Book comes down to us from men who were held by a belief in the literal truth of the whole Bible. In so far as it has been an effective manual for ordinary people, it has been on the strength of an absolute dogma in their minds as to the "Word of God." That dogma has in a vague and somewhat insensible way lost its hold on the common mind. It has not the absolute and simple authority which in religion is a necessity for the little-educated. Few of the general public have thought very much about the matter, but all the more they are influenced by that which has percolated through to them from the more learned, loosening what before was firm and tight, confusing and complicating what before was starkly plain. This has been brought home to me as I have sat at sing-songs and have heard a coon-song sung entitled "The Preacher and the Bear." With apologies to the easily-shocked I will quote. The hero of the song is a coloured minister who, against his conscience, went out shooting on a Sunday, and, after good sport, on returning home was met by a grizzly bear. Taking refuge up a tree this was his prayer:

O Lord, who delivered Daniel from the lions' den,
Also Jonah from the tummy of the whale—and then
Three Hebrew chilluns from the fiery furnace,
As the good Book do declare—
O Lord, if you can't help me, don't help that grizzly bear!

Here is an epitome of a far-spreading incredulity about the Bible. It is the higher criticism in its crudest popular form, and men are at the mercy of it. I have known a mess of officers engage in argument about the Bible with a sceptical Scots doctor, cleverer than they. As old-fashioned believers in the Bible they had to admit to being thoroughly "strafed" in the argument, yet they had no way out, such as an intelligent understanding of the Bible affords. One at least of them maintained stoutly that nevertheless he was going to stick to the old view, however indefensible. Such men are not free intellectually to follow the movements of religious revival. They are immobilised by the dead weight of Biblical literalism.

Yet if the main verdict to which I have committed myself is to be radically accounted for, it is necessary to reach deeper reasons than any I have mentioned. I sympathise with those who have high hopes of the good effects of Church and Prayer Book and Bible-teaching reforms. Yet such are relatively superficial matters. The main reason for the comparative absence of religious revival among men at the front is that we all have been overtaken by the cataclysm of war in a condition of great poverty towards God.

VI

War, when it breaks in on peace, reveals in a fierce light the condition of men in peace. It would be ungrateful and disloyal not to acclaim the main sound heart of our country which this war has revealed. It would be treasonable to the great company of good men and true—not least out of the school and university world most familiar to the writer—who have risen to "the day" and have gladly given their all. Yet, after generous allowance for that, a great poverty of allegiance to God has been laid bare. Indirectly, in the answers made to the claims of duty, honour, service, and self-sacrifice, He has been acknowledged, but of direct devotion to Him as the one and pre-eminent reality there has been little. After all, can it be denied that the war has found us devoted rather to the idols of money, pleasure, and appetite than to God and His righteousness? We have had to be aroused from a great sensual preoccupation with worldly traffic. "As it was in the days of Noah," so in a measure it has been to-day: "as we ate and drank, and bought and sold and planted and builded, the flood has come upon us" and has all but swept us away. At home, as the thinly-veiled wantonness of some of our weekly illustrated papers reminds us in the field, it seems that a mass of self-pleasing and luxurious folk cannot yet find an escape out of the prison-house of Vanity Fair, though thousands bleed and die by their side. In the field, the mind and manner of a gross peace-life is kept alive by pictures of smirking nudities placarded in dug-outs and billets, and the farther back from the front one travels, as the hot breath of war grows more tepid, the more heavy grows the atmosphere of materialistic indulgence. That *God minds* is hardly thought of, for at home and abroad we have been carried into war in a peace-condition of great heedlessness of Him. And the strains and cost and dangers of war will not scare men out of their forgetfulness. The heart of man is incorrigible by fear. God, if He is little regarded in peace, is hard to come nigh to in war. If religion in peace and prosperity has not been full of His praise—of joy *in Him*, it is something to which adversity must drive men, and they think it as such a little disreputable, and many of the best men, richly gifted with manly excellences, tend to leave it on one side.

Yet "I am not ashamed of the Gospel of Christ." We can adopt the ringing note of St. Paul's defiance. For the Christian religion does not spring primarily out of human anxiety and need. It is not an expedient which may be left on one side till the hour of need arises. That many men should think thus of it shows that it has been widely forgotten, misunderstood, or never known.

VII

The Christian religion is salvation because it starts from what God is. Everything in it of human benefit and satisfaction is a bye-product flowing from the fact that it gives to men a focus for their devotion and attention not in themselves but in God. Its main motive is not self- but God-regarding. It draws men out of the entanglement into which they fall through temporising with their own needs, and constrains them to attend to God's need—His need of them. For the Christian, God is not some shadowy supreme Being at the back of the universe, or a name given to the sum of things. God is the Person Who made, and loves, and therefore wants His children. Hence Christian prayer primarily is grateful and loving acknowledgment of what God is, and only secondarily the expression of anxiety, or the "putting in" of this or that claim for what we want.

That is the conclusion which war experience drives home. The special strain and pressure of war cannot elicit from the majority of men the religion which is occupied with the saving of self. The spiritual law is that we find our life by losing it, not by saving it. In a vague and unexpressed way, as they show again and again by their cheerfulness and unconcernedness, hosts of men in this war have laid hold on this law. They have found a purpose to which to cleave, something to give themselves away for. Only it is hardly acknowledged, but rather lies below the level of mental apprehension and expression. It is the function of Christianity to raise this unacknowledging trustfulness and self-giving out of dumb subconsciousness, and to give to it speech, and to crown it with the glory of fully human self-devotion. It is its part to declare that it is God Whom they find in the offering of themselves, His love in which they can lose themselves, His purpose to which they can cleave, His will to be done—and that to give Him joy is the supreme end of man.

This is the religion which sustains in war, because possessed in peace. And it is so little prevalent—that is, so little in any one's *conscious* possession—in war just because God, and His love, and His desire have been so little in men's thoughts in peace. Let peace return—let the strain of war be lifted from a unit as it goes back into rest, or from an individual as he goes on leave, and the life of indulgence, without an object except self, threatens to repossess the soul. In the same way it is peace rather than war, health rather than sickness, youth rather than age, which really test the reality of our Christianity, when, without the shame of being driven thereto by need, a man can rejoice in God, and with full powers be made the instrument of His will.

VIII

There is then little conscious and articulate Christianity at the front, and yet there are profoundly Christian characteristics in what men are and do and endure, who have never known or do not understand or have forgotten the Christian religion. What, then, is this strangely honoured and yet neglected thing? Does it exist? Is it there for men were they to awake to it?

This utterly searching war justifies the critical temper which passes previous allegiances and acceptances under revision and judgment. I may be forgiven, then, for saying that I do not think that Christianity as at present expressed and presented to men in the Church (in the widest sense of the word) is *prima facie* that which can win and possess them. It would be a big task and unsuited to the conditions under which I write to argue this out. What needs discussion is how much of natural religion has been absorbed into the accumulated deposit from the past which we call traditional Christianity, with the effect of disguising and overlaying in it those specifically Christian elements, which make Christianity not only a salvation from sin or from hell, but from the morbid and even contemptible in religion. Those elements can never be clearly abstracted and used by themselves, for Christianity was not a thing rounded and completed, and deposited upon the world *in vacuo*, but was as a seed sown, which grows by drawing into itself the nourishment of soil and atmosphere. There always must be elements of natural religion interfused with the Christian religion, for though not evolved out of natural religion, but rather coming to it as a deliverance, Christianity is the crown and fulfilment and corroboration of the good and the true in natural religion. It is not a question of clear separation and abstraction, but of distinction, emphasis, and proportion. I believe that things not characteristically Christian have acquired a disproportionate place in our religion as handed down to us.

I suggest (but will not work it out here) that many of the hymns in use are evidence of this, and that is why so often they do not ring true. I also believe that an unhistorical use of the Bible has proved a distorting influence. From early Christian days Scripture, which is a story of a process and growth containing many stages and imperfections, has been treated as something timeless and absolute. In particular, the partial answers to the problem of suffering to which the Jews in their development were led, have been made to bear weights heavier than they can sustain. Some of the Psalms, for instance, over-emphasise the connection between righteousness and immunity from misfortune. They can be used to justify a calculating and self-saving religion which is below the level of Christ's religion. A soldier, recently wounded on the Somme, handed to me at a dressing-station a small copy of the 91st Psalm as his religious handbook. Yet by itself the 91st Psalm, though a wonderful expression of trust in God, promises a security to which our Lord, and others akin to Him in spirit, have not put their seal. He did not ask—He resisted the temptation to ask—that no evil should happen unto Him, nor that angels should bear Him in their hands lest He should hurt His foot against a stone. He would not have men set their face in the day of battle in the assurance that, though a thousand should fall beside them and ten thousand at their right hand, the same lot would not come nigh them.

I think, too, that Christianity fails to make its characteristic appeal through the Church, owing to two prevalent "isms"—ecclesiasticism and subjectivism—both of which may be said to be the being primarily occupied in religion with something other than God. I doubt whether any Church-party advantage can be scored by any one in this matter. Roughly speaking, the weakness of Catholic Christianity is to get involved in the little things of "mint and anise and cummin"; whilst the weakness of Protestantism is to become absorbed in the luxuries of one's own religious experiences. The upshot of either is the same, namely, to be very religious, and yet to forget the living God. I remember being very much startled by an eminently pious Anglo-Catholic undergraduate at Oxford saying to me, "The fact is, I am not interested in God the Father." It is unwise to argue from one instance, but I seem to see there a symptom of a widespread and tragic estrangement of institutional Christianity from the mind of Christ. But I doubt whether things are much better on the other side of the ecclesiastical street, where so often the worship of God has downgraded into sitting and listening to sentimental music on Pleasant Sunday Afternoons. Single instances are misleading, but I can never dismiss the belief that there is something radically wrong with the world of religion of which the representative was a Chapel, in my old parish at Leeds, that indulged in a "fruit-banquet" on Good Friday. Right through organised Christianity of all kinds there is, I think, a great absence of the real Christian thing.

IX

But this brings round again the question, "What is this Christian thing?" What are the characteristic and specific elements which, though they cannot be nakedly abstracted from other elements, yet have to be kept salient amid everything else? What is the Christianity which is generally not in the conscious possession of men at the front, and yet receives the seal of their glorious excellences? What is the Christianity which lies hidden by traditional disguise and contemporary practice? Where is it to be found?

X

At any rate, in the religion of Jesus of Nazareth. We are blessed by the privilege, given to us by the work of realistic historians, of going to Him as our real Brother. We can study the religion of this Man. It was rooted first and last in one dominant reality—the Father and His will. From the first sight given to us of Him as a boy and onwards He was rich in one thing—He was rich towards God. He looked at the world without insensibility to its pain, without evasion of its evil—rather with uniquely sensitive insight into both— as God's world and the scene of God's sovereign activity. And He expected others to share His view. He was repeatedly astonished to find those around Him heedless of the air which He drew in with open mouth, blind to what He saw, deaf to what He heard, unelated by His joy. He was surprised to find them strangely and otherwise absorbed, with hearts elsewhere centred than in God. He expected to find them united to God in a loving loyalty. He found them in a spiritual adultery.

This unshared absorption of Jesus was not the fruit of adversity nor a resort in disappointment. He was not driven to it by anxiety. It came first for Him in peace, in full health, and youth and powers. His was a house which was built in fine weather upon a rock, so that when the storms of adversity beat on it, it stood firm. His religion stood the severest test, namely, the quiet of normal and uneventful days. It was ready for the strain of a campaign. He emerged out of the peace of Nazareth prepared for enterprise. For the Father to Him was not only the object of immobile worship and delight—not only a Name to be hallowed, but was He Who called Him out to a venture for His kingdom and the doing of His will.

That was how Jesus came among men. He came calling men to a great adventure, to non-calculating and self-regardless co-operation with the active energy and will of the Father. How much He knew beforehand of whither that will would lead Him can never be known. To suppose that He knew all and saw the end in the beginning and had no steps in the dark to take, would be to deny to Him the essential element of human faith and trust, which is that it has to step out beyond the light of knowledge into the darkness of uncertainty. On the other hand, to suppose that He knew nothing, is to deny to Him that humanly heroic resolution with which He set His face to tread the path which led Him to suffering. In our ignorance let us grip this certainty, that for Him the one sufficient thing was that the Father knew all things—the times and the seasons, the cup to be drunk, the will to be done and the final outcome. That was enough for Him and must be enough for us.

This religion of Jesus then is that to which all can turn, as their hearts are full beyond expression with proud and thankful sorrow for the great company of those who have trustfully given themselves to death for others. Jesus is the Word, that is, the full and crowning expression of that which is hardly articulate in others. His open-eyed self-consecration to do the will of the Father seals and ratifies their confused yet steadfast devotion. He is first among many brethren, giving full utterance to their dumb trustfulness. In a world of mixed and partial motives He is the absolute and unmitigated lover of God—loving with all His mind and soul and strength, freely hazarding all upon the Father.

XI

Is not that enough? This simple element—this religion of Jesus—is it not the one thing needful, possessed of which men may slough off all else in the traditional deposits of Christianity? Yes, would certainly be the answer if the men of His day had in fact been so possessed, and if men were so possessed to-day. What was actual in Him was, is, in fact, unrealised in them. He did find, of old, fellow-adventurers to share His enterprise. But they could not share it to the end. He could love God wholly, they only partially. He had to leave them, and they Him; He to do the will of the Father, they to fail to do it. He alone could not only announce but fulfil the first and great commandment; they in the end could only be defied and broken by it.

So it was proved. And it is a result which any honest man can verify for himself. As I have tried to show elsewhere,[1] the most rigorously human and non-miraculous view of Jesus and the Gospels leads to this point, to what may be called the porch where Peter wept, where the silence of God broods over the tragedy of human failure.

FOOTNOTES:

[1] *The Mind of the Disciples* (Macmillan).

XII

"But the third day He rose again." Peter was not left in the porch, nor are we. His broken hope was remade by the One fully trusted in by Jesus only—by the "God and Father of the Lord Jesus Christ."[2]

The Christian thing which we look for is the Good News of *God* in Christ. It is not only the religion *of* Jesus our Brother, but religion *in* Jesus, in Him revealing God to men. It is not only His human richness towards God, but in Him the richness of God towards men. It is the Cross not only as the climax of free loving self-offering to the Father, but as itself the laying bare of the Father's heart—it is *God* reconciling the world unto Himself.

It is this—the revelation of God in Christ—of which the experience of the war shows we are above all else in the world in need. God, not merely assented to as a mysterious "One above," at the back of things, but God, known and delighted in, in terms of Jesus Christ. It is one great light which we need to walk in—the light of the knowledge of what God is, as it shines upon the face of Jesus Christ. The specific Christian thing that makes Christianity salvation is not—as so many men in the army think—just goodness nor negative and kill-joy propriety, but the fact that *in the ardent, venturesome, and self-regardless sacrifice of Jesus, we see the Love of God Himself coming out to win the souls of men.*

Everything else follows from that, and comes second to it as first—all that follows from God's love being holy, and from men being unholy, all that is meant by Christian experience, all that is involved in the activities of prayer and service. Men have to begin from, and ever keep rallying round, the truth of what God is as made known in Christ—treating the truth as no matter of course, but as the disclosure which in this strange world seems nearly too good to be true.

For there is no reconciliation between the facts of the world and the Absolute of philosophy or the highly attributed Supreme Being of natural religion. One thing alone can meet the passion of men—whether imposed upon them or self-inflicted—it is the passion of God in Christ whereby His Love works out its victory. That alone can harness to itself the vitality and heroism of men, which else will riot away in waste or flag in disillusion. That alone can be the constraining object of their joy and praise, and the satisfaction of their adventurous devotion.

FOOTNOTES:

[2] 1 Peter i. 3.

XIII

There has been in this war a wonderful display of the heroism of men. But their thoughts about God and religion are for the most part at a level below the highest in themselves. They have come to themselves in giving themselves away. But they think that religion is mostly concerned with self-saving. They tend to recognise most easily the signs of God's favour in this or that instance of safety or escape. This means that they do not think of God in terms of Christ, but that they think of Him as outside the trouble and pain and cost of life, and in the immunity of heaven. They do not think of Him as involved in the risks and agonies of the world. Though they do not formulate it to themselves, the glories of human nature go beyond anything they know of the divine. For them God is less wonderful than man. A fine soldier protested to me lately about the service which was read at the funeral of a very brave officer, "Why say more than 'here is a very gallant soldier'?" as though there were nothing in the Author of our being akin to the gallantry in man. Not that such a man would deny the idea, but that he and the rest are not possessed by joy in its truth. Men of our race do not deny greatly, but then neither do they joyfully assert. They have not received the good news of God in Christ.

XIV

We all need to be so possessed before peace comes back. For peace, as I have said, is the real test of our religion, not war. We have been plunged into war, rejoicing little in God. We have got to put Him and His will and desire first before peace returns. Or else the thought of Him will sink out of our attention, and we shall return to the getting of gain and to self-service in a mood of perpetual postponement. God will come last again. He did so in the minds of soldiers at the beginning of the war. Often they looked upon chaplains as no more than preliminary undertakers. At the beginning of the war, officers in my old regiment, in the friendliest way, asked me what there was to do as a chaplain except burial duties. Clearly they thought of *life* as something apart from God.

What is needed is a new joy in God as Love and Purpose, here and now. Need, whether the pressure of sickness or danger or anxiety or age or guilt, will often operate in turning the heart God-ward. The sense of being thrown in entire dependence upon God can be the God-given turning-point in a man's life and an end to his godlessness. But need will never provide the lasting religious motive which sets the chord of what is noblest in men vibrating within them. The peculiar glory of the Christian religion is that it provides that motive—it is the motive of God's need. He wants us, for He loves us. He is love.

I have found myself at the front pressed to ask men why they should have to do with religion. Is it because they are on active service and exposed to danger and liable to death? Is that to be the constraining motive? And, in particular, why pray? Is it to express their natural sense of need, their desire for security and support? Is that to be the main impulse? I try to answer these questions by asking them another question: 'Why do they write home?' What keeps them at it in the damp dug-outs with the indelible pencil running smudgily over the paper? Why do some men write every day? Is it for what they can get—the cakes, the fags? Does the constraining motive lie in their own need? It does not. It lies in the joy which letters bring to loving hearts at home. Likewise there is joy in Heaven when one forgetful wayward son turns in heart thither homewards.

For God loves us and therefore wants us and desires to use us. It is what He is which is the saving motive of our religion. Every other motive, however natural, is tainted with morbidity, and can never long possess the eager hearts of men nor be their glory in the full tide of life. But in God they can glory as they see what He is, at work with purposes of holy love in the venture of creation; and this they can see in Christ, living, suffering, dying, rising, and alive for evermore; or else Christianity is nothing in the world. That is the pure metal of our glorious religion, which the fierce fires of war must refine out of its traditional alloy. That is the great golden secret uttered in Christ— God, all-suffering and all-faithful love, calling out into active alliance the like qualities in His children for the accomplishment of His will on earth as in heaven.

XV

We need in peace the free and conscious realisation of that of which men are perforce, and dumbly, aware in war. It is that there is something going on in the world which demands primary allegiance, and the putting second of every self-interest. At the front men hardly know what it is. They are suspicious of rhetoric and unreality in talk about liberty and international equity, and right against might. They only know—a wonderful majority of them—that something great and righteous wants them and requires of them their help. So, reluctantly, with grumblings and insistent longing for it all to be over, and yet with the inalienable joy of doing the right thing, they obstinately endure. We can say, without apportioning right wholesale to the Allies or wrong wholesale to Germany, that, however dimly aware of it, they are 'seeking first the Kingdom of God and His Righteousness.'

Can they maintain this allegiance in peace despite every seduction which will rush to recapture their souls? That is the great question which all who call themselves Christians should be considering on their knees while the war is still raging.

The answer lies in a great measure with the Church. She has to enlist in her warfare for the kingdom of God—the war which is never over—that capacity in men for service and suffering which the war has disclosed. How can this be? Would that I had no uncertain answer to utter! I fling these cries out to comrades in the Lord that we may provoke one another to find the answer. The answer cannot be merely an intellectual solution. It must be spelt out in terms of costly devotion.

Some things are clear. First, the Church has to acknowledge that she is not the kingdom of God but the means to it as an end. There are, I think, a great many carts and horses to be changed round into their right relations. Religious observances and organisations—all the whole apparatus of religion—have come to be looked upon as ends in themselves, whereas they are means to an end beyond themselves. People think that the clergy's one concern is the success of ecclesiastical activities and institutions. We clergy think so ourselves! It is not for her own interests, which are by themselves incurably too small to evoke the heroic in men, that the Church is in the world. She is in the world to change the world, so that its whole extent may be filled with the glory of God, and may become worthy of the eternal destiny of the souls of men. Hers is a high and costly venture. She has strongholds to storm—the entrenchments where the forces of private-mindedness and apathy and money-worship are dug in. In the attempt she can exhaust to its depths the capacity which is in men for dauntless sacrifice.

Secondly, if the Church's conception of her own interests must be changed, so must the individual's conception of personal religion. Self-preoccupation is as fatal to the latter as to the former. Personal piety is travestied by being thought to be a respectable prudence here for the sake of a reward hereafter. It is not a careful self-salvation at all. Rather it is a salvation from self. It is the being lost to self in devotion and service to God and one's fellow-men.

Lastly, if these changes are to be they depend on one thing—a new vision of God in Christ, such as shall be for Church and individual the over-mastering counter-attraction to self. What the world needs is theocracy. That is, not the imposition of ecclesiastical shackles upon secular life, but the consecration of all life, with all its ever-multiplying treasures of knowledge and power, to one object—the glory of God. If so, then God, as the centre and magnet of consecration, must be all vitally apprehended. He must fill the horizon of the soul. He must be the delight of men, to draw them out of themselves into childlike selflessness, so that as children they may enter into the Kingdom.

XVI

There are objections, I know, which arise in the mind to this insistence on God and the will or kingdom on which He is at work in the world, and they must be faced. It is easy, I feel, to speak of the will of God in general terms. But what does it mean in particular? Can it be known or defined? Is it practicable?

I remember being puzzled by a great religious teacher to whom I owe much—Father Kelly of the Society of the Sacred Mission, Kelham. It was almost comic to me that in the same breath he would urge (1) that the one thing needful was faith in God and in the will which He is accomplishing in His world, and—with equal energy—(2) that no one could say what in the world that will is. It reminded me of those philosophers who liken the metaphysical pursuit of the Absolute to Lewis Carroll's *Hunting of the Snark*.

But there is something essential here. Christian faith in God and in His will is not sight, else it were no venture. It does not bring with it a particularised programme to meet all the changing and complex circumstances of life. It does not carry with it anticipatory knowledge. Yet it is not an agnostic gazing into the mist of heaven. It is the looking unto Jesus. There is light—light on His Cross, telling of the love and will and desire of God Who is marching on.

Given the attitude of faith in God and the belief that He is at work in human affairs, the practical corollaries have to be worked out by the exertion of our faculties. If God and His will be the end of our endeavour and the object of our co-operation, then the means towards the end and the ways of co-operation must be arrived at, step by step, by effort and experiment, by science and common sense. The endeavour to do God's will, will disclose what that will is.

After all, in every sphere of human relationships, whether in home or neighbourhood or business or municipality or commonwealth, what is lacking is not the knowledge of what the kingdom of God requires, but the will and motive and power to accomplish it. We are not short of knowledge; rather we are weighed down by the power derived from new knowledge, for want of an end other than our own selves to which to consecrate it. The means for transforming life and suffusing it with new radiance abound as never before. It is the will which is lacking. If we will lift up any department of life to God in the faith that He cares about it and has desires for it, the next step to be taken will be apparent to conscience and reason.

XVII

Akin to the difficulty that the will of God is inscrutable and hard to know, is the protest that to speak of Him as at work in the world to bring in His kingdom, is remote from the actualities of daily life. As I have walked about in Flanders, turning over thoughts about the onward movement of God's purposes in the world, I have met those matchless monuments of patient and unchanging daily toil, the peasants working in the fields. Harnessed into the perpetual cycle of seed time and harvest, what can this talk of movements and purposes in the great world be to them? Is enthusiasm for the Kingdom of God possible only for those who are so removed from the drudgery of existence that they can sit in the exhausted air of committee rooms and talk about it? Or is it that under God's heaven and close to the soil men know better? Is there no room for great expectations in those pressed down into the thick of things?

There is telling truth here, but it is not the last word. The old man in the fields—or is it the old wrinkled woman doing more than one man's work?—knows that. They know that life cannot fully be measured by the gauge of the individual's daily round. A word will bring pride and light to their eyes. It is 'Vive la France!' They are citizens of a world wider than their fields. They belong to 'La Patrie.' Their common tasks count—only a little—but they do count in the world of great events. Life is monotonous and cyclical, and yet it is more than that. Great changes do arrive in days of crisis and convulsion—yes, in days of judgment, and the victims of changelessness are caught up by movement. They are awakened out of the sleep of humdrum existence, and are asked to give proof, and proudly do give proof, that, plodders though they be, they belong to no mean city.

This is true in the sphere of patriotism. It is true in the wider sphere of the Kingdom of God. The difficulty here considered is one of the products of our incorrigible individualism in religion. Christianity is not narrow preoccupation with 'my soul.' It is an entrance into a sphere as wide as the world. It is membership in a universal society which is concerned with great causes and astir with deep movements. And be the individual never so anchored in the daily and local necessities of existence, he can nevertheless share with loyalty and pride and prayer and service in the fortunes and onward march of the commonwealth of Christ.

XVIII

There is also the objection to an insistence upon the will of God in accomplishment in this world, that there is so much in the New Testament which declares (and, as we have seen in the last paragraph, experience seems largely to corroborate the view) that the Kingdom of God does not come in this world but in the next. I refer (only I dislike using a word which few soldiers at the front will understand) to New Testament "apocalyptic," which seems to present a vision of this world as immediately to pass away in catastrophe and of the arrival of another order of things.

It is certainly very perplexing that there seems to be so little in the New Testament outside of the Gospels which is plainly on all fours with the first part of the Lord's Prayer. At the front the Lord's Prayer—as the one island of religious ground, amid marshes of ignorance, common to Englishmen—is the padres' great stand-by. It declares better than any words which we can frame what distinguishes the Christian religion from others—that it begins with and glories in what God is Whose Name is to be hallowed, and Whose kingdom is in arrival and Whose will is in accomplishment not only in heaven but *on earth*. But elsewhere in the New Testament the *terrain*, as it were, of these wonderful happenings seems to be changed, and to lie in the hereafter.

It is very hard to say anything simply and shortly about this.

At any rate it is no good blinking the fact that the New Testament expectation of an immediate ending of this world was mistaken.[3]

Yet there remains the reasonable faith—surely burnt into us by the fires of war, surely revealed to us in apocalyptic vision—that this world is but a part of another, and that the other gives to this and to its concerns their supreme importance.

We need to be two-eyed here. It is a one-eyed view to hold that because this life is a pilgrimage to another and this world is passing away, therefore nothing matters here and nothing is happening here. It is equally one-eyed to shut out the goal whither we all journey, and to concentrate on the affairs of this life as alone and sufficiently important.

The whole view is that through the entire order—here and there—the will of God is at work, and His Kingdom in arrival, but that their full result and accomplishment lies beyond this world. Here are the partial and unfinished stages, there the end whither they lead. To fall back on metaphor, a city is in the building, a whole righteous social order—a kingdom of souls. The building is going on now,—in Birmingham and Bermondsey,—and that gives eternal importance to their perishing and trivial affairs. What whole structure is being built, and how much of Birmingham and Bermondsey can be built into it, is only partially known now. It is partially known here, as days of testing and catastrophe break in on periods of monotony, and lay bare their soul. But full knowledge lies in the future—the great and final 'Day shall declare it.'

XIX

There is also the objection that too hard things have been said here about the turning to God under pressure of anxiety, and the expression in prayer of the natural desire for safety. After all, as a Jesuit fellow-padre reminded me at the front, Our Lord at His hour of trial, when "exceeding sorrowful even unto death," prayed in agony. And further it is plain that prayer to Him, and as He would have it be to others, was far more than a trustful harmony of self with the will of the Father. He urged men to take their *requests* to God. "Ask and ye shall receive." I can imagine that the conception of prayer at times of emergency, as suggested in earlier pages, might be so full of resignation as to be reduced to the fatalism extraordinarily prevalent at the front—"If it 'its yer, it 'its yer," as the men say. Are we not to ask not to be hit?

It is nearly enough to recall the Lord's Prayer in regard to this objection. As I have said, men on service widely associate prayer with the expression of need or anxiety. To restrict prayer thus is to begin the Lord's Prayer half-way through, at "Give us this day our daily bread." It is a question of order and emphasis. Christian prayer begins with God. It turns away from self to the glory of God. It begins with praise and acclamation—the glad acknowledgment of what God is and is doing. It is only in the second place and because of what God is—because He is our Father and is at work to bring in His kingdom and has a will for us and for all—that the prayer which expresses our need comes in aright.

Therefore I would say to a man going into battle—"Pray now if never before. Set God before you as you see Him, as you can clearly apprehend Him, in Christ. He is your Father, you are His son, however unworthy. Lift up your heart to Him Who, in and through all the turmoil around you, presses onward with the business of His kingdom and the fulfilment of His heart's desire. And commit all to Him. In trustful intimacy give utterance to your longing to be brought through the perilous hour for service in His kingdom to the glory of His Name. Commit all to Him, asking forgiveness. He knows what you have need of in life or in death—and let the rest go!"

For such prayer in the Name of Christ—that is, prayer in accordance with His mind and founded on the character of God as made known in Him—there awaits undiscovered and unexhausted resources of power. So Jesus told men. So Christian experience testifies. We have to pray truly Christ-wise, not asking for stones to be made bread, not seeking to be hidden from life's storms, but to be brought through them in faithful endurance.[4]

We have to pray as Christ prayed in Gethsemane in fellowship with His sufferings. But we have also to pray as knowing the power of His

Resurrection. We have to rise in faith to claim the supernatural power which neither He used nor we may use merely for self-preservation, which yet is to be set free in the service of the kingdom.

Prayer in the Name of Christ is not only the prayer of resignation, based on the self-committal of Jesus our Brother into the hands of the Father. Such would ever tend, as uttered by our trembling faith, towards fatalism. But it is also prayer in the Name of Him "Who was declared to be the Son of God with power by the resurrection of the dead, even Jesus Christ our Lord." It is the prayer of power—that power which was at Jesus' command, and was therefore the subject of His temptation, and was drawn upon by the faith of sufferers and yet was unused by Jesus to save Himself. This power is the power of God. It is "the exceeding greatness of His power, according to that working of the strength of His might which He wrought in Christ, when He raised Him from the dead and made Him to sit at His right hand in the heavenly places."

Here are heights where the air is charged with potentiality of new life, hardly dreamt of by our faith on its low stagnant levels. Here are heights to be stormed by faithful unself-seeking love. This way lies deliverance and new creation, and the breaking of prison bars and the turning of our captivity such as shall fill all our mouths with laughter.

A few know that these words are not rhetorical. They know, with St. Paul, the riches of the glory of Christ's inheritance in the saints. Such was Mary Slessor, pioneer missionary in West Africa, the leaves of whose biography I happened to turn over as I was writing these pages. She had frequently to take journeys through forests with leopards swarming around her. She wrote: "I did not use to believe the story of Daniel in the lions' den until I had to take some of these awful marches, and then I knew it was true and that it was written for my comfort. Many a time I walked along praying 'O God of Daniel, shut their mouths,' and He did."[5]

This is the prayer of faith. It is the prayer which asks "not to be hit." It is more than resignation, it is the prayer of power. It believes that there are hardly-tapped powers and possibilities in God for those who seek first His kingdom and righteousness. We do not know much about such prayer in our present spiritual sickness. But it is there, a weapon to be wielded by dauntless, simple faith. There is an inheritance to be claimed by little-loving sons, who yet are sons—"heirs of God and joint heirs with Christ, if so be that we suffer with Him."

[4] Prayer after the mind of our Lord depends greatly on how we think of Him. The following lines, written by a barrister, are, I think, a wholesome corrective of that which is too soft in our conventional thought about our Saviour. Despite a false or partial note here and there, they are nearer to Him than the thought underlying the first verse of the hymn—a great favourite among the men owing to its tune—"Jesu, Lover of my Soul." At any rate they suggest the right association of ideas in which our Lord should live in the mind of a young man:

Jesus, Whose lot with us was cast,
Who saw it out, from first to last:
Patient and fearless, tender, true,
Carpenter, vagabond, felon, Jew:
Whose humorous eye took in each phase
Of full rich life this world displays,
Yet evermore kept fast in view
The far-off goal it leads us to:

Who, as your hour neared, did not fail—
The world's fate trembling in the scale—
With your half-hearted band to dine,
And chat across the bread and wine:
Then went out firm to face the end,
Alone, without a single friend:
Who felt, as your last words confessed,
Wrung from a proud unflinching breast
By hours of dull ignoble pain,
Your whole life's fight was fought in vain:
Would I could win and keep and feel
That heart of love, that spirit of steel.

I would not to Thy bosom fly
To slink off till the storms go by.
If you are like the man you were
You'ld turn with scorn from such a prayer,
Unless from some poor workhouse crone,
Too toil-worn to do aught but moan.
Flog me and spur me, set me straight
At some vile job I fear and hate:
Some sickening round of long endeavour,
No light, no rest, no outlet ever:
All at a pace that must not slack,

Tho' heart would burst and sinews crack:
Fog in one's eyes, the brain a-swim,
A weight like lead in every limb,
And a raw pit that hurts like hell
Where once the light breath rose and fell:
Do you but keep me, hope or none,
Cheery and staunch till all is done,
And, at the last gasp, quick to lend
One effort more to serve a friend.

And when—for so I sometimes dream—
I've swum the dark, the silent stream,
So cold, it takes the breath away,
That parts the dead world from the day,
And see upon the further strand
The lazy, listless angels stand,
And with their frank and fearless eyes
The comrades whom I most did prize:
Then, clean, unburdened, careless, cool,
I'll saunter up from that grim pool,
And join my friends: then you'll come by,
The Captain of our Company:
Call me out, look me up and down,
And pass me through without a frown,
With half a smile, but never a word—
And so I shall have met my Lord.

[5] *Mary Slessor of Calabar: Pioneer Missionary*, p. 106. Hodder & Stoughton.

XX

There is also the objection that the view implied in the preceding pages leaves out or passes over too lightly our need as sinners in the sight of God all Holy. Is not our need for forgiveness to impel us towards God? Is not our need—our need in anxiety, our need in guiltiness—to be a motive in our religion?

Yes, a motive, but not the motive. It is a question of order. What must come first is not our need, whether as anxious or guilty, but God's need, or else our religion will be at the level of natural religion and below the Christian level. It is because men are poor towards God and think coldly and ungenerously of Him that they 'are not worrying about their sins.' Men are not sorry for sin (except with the seedy remorse of 'the morning after') until their sin has come into contact with love. The more vital a young man is, the less will he brood in self-regard over his wrongdoing. "Anyhow, I have lived," he will say. But if it comes home to him what his wrongdoing has done to another who loves him, then he begins to be sorry. "I didn't care," he will say, "for myself. I had my fling. But now I see that what I did has broken my mother's heart. I wish to God I hadn't done it."

Our religion must begin from God. It must spring out of love fuller and more hungry than our desirous hearts. It must spring out of love, not—how could it?—out of our love for God, but out of His love for us. If God's love for us, manifested in the utterly real and suffering love of Jesus, and in no insipid fancy of our sentimental moments, wins its way past our guard and over the barriers of self, hatred of sin and sorrow for sin will follow. But it is a question of order: first, what God is; second, what we are. The more vivid the first is to a man, the more inevitable his candid consciousness of the second. The more he is taken captive by the assurance that God is his Father, the more glaring it will be to him that he is an unworthy son. And the more men set out to give effect to their sonship in service for the kingdom of God, the more they will realise their strange impotence. The dreadful hiatus between aspiration and performance, between acknowledged and realised ideals will widen. The eager impulse to disregard self and to serve God with love and praise and joy, will be found horridly at variance with a natural and rooted impulse towards self-devotion and indulgence. The worship and praise of God, not only in thought and word but in deed, will stumble and fall short of its goal—and then the tears of tragic failure will start and the cry of despair ring out. It was so with Peter in the porch and Paul beaten down in bondage under the Law. "Who shall deliver us from the body of this death?"

I think there is no fear but that, if we do set out to put into practice our inheritance as sons of God, we shall come to the Cross of Christ in genuine

"Rock-of-ages" fashion, bringing nothing to it in the end, except our lovelessness. His, after all and in fact, was the one, free, utterly loving and obedient offering of self to the Father. He did something others could not do—He died for them, and in Him and through Him alone did they come unto the Holy Father. I cannot work it out here, but along this way I seem to travel home into the great evangel of the Atonement.

Only, I plead, this propitiatory work of Christ must come second in the imagination, and His Love-of-God-revealing work first. And I think in the course of the history of Christianity an inversion has come about. In hymns and liturgies the *prima facie* and predominant emphasis seems rather to rest on our sinfulness than on God's goodness. Before they do anything else the Prayer Book, as it is at present used, asks men to embark on the overloaded phrases of the General Confession. I know that this may be justified by arguing that the Prayer Book assumes that the other parts of the Christian religion are in the minds of 'the faithful' members of the Church. But this assumption is unwarranted as regards the mass of soldiers whom we keep on inviting to use the more or less mutilated forms of Morning and Evening Prayer.

And even when we come to the Eucharist, though everything can be found in it, I often wonder whether there the Church has not come to lay more stress upon the Cross as the offering for sin than as the disclosure of the Divine pity for the sinner. If so, is it that too much has been taken for granted, namely, the Love of God which alone can evoke sorrow for sin and be worthy of the offering for sin? Has familiarity tended to disguise and overlay the wonder-compelling revelation of God? In the Eucharist has He been thought of rather as the Father sitting back in reception of placation, than as the Father Who, while we are a great way off, runs out to fall on our neck and bring us home?

I think that a re-ordering is needed. For Christianity, stressed as it appears to be at present, will never catch the souls of men. I think of the flying boys who, more than any one else, are winning our battles (I have been chaplain to a squadron of them for a little time). They are far from unsinful, but they will nevertheless, I am sure, not *begin* with the avowal "that there is no health in them"; they will not sing "that they are weary of earth and laden with their sins." For as they live almost gaily and unconcernedly on the edge of things, they know that that is not the primary truth about themselves. Yet Christ, if in Him they see the all-hazarding and all-enduring Love of God, can win the love and worship of their eager hearts. He can catch those living creatures alive.

There must be a re-ordering and simplification and correction of emphasis. It is possible, now that historical science is unravelling the Bible and Church history, and extricating from their many levels and complexities what is simple and specific in the glorious truths of God and of man in Christ. Some exaggerations must be sloughed off. I think a little of the sepia, for instance, that was in the brush of Paul must be washed away. Has not he, or rather have not the great men of his school, over-obsessed us with the dogma, derived from Scriptural literalism, of human corruption flowing from Adam?

There is, by contrast, a more radiant and yet as realistic view of the world as Christ saw it, to be recovered. Some of His glories, dimmed by the veil of inadequate conceptions in the minds of His witnesses, will shine as never before, as the Holy Spirit takes of Him and shows it unto us.

XXI

Finally, I would say a word about the charge of pessimism which this report from the front may evoke. Both pessimism and optimism are rather moods in us than qualities which really belong to the facts of a situation. The main point is to try to get down to reality and not to flinch. Anyhow, I do not feel pessimistic about our holy and glorious religion. Far otherwise. It is coming again. Actualities at the front, as I try to learn from them, do seem to me to show a very widespread and deep ignorance of the good news of God in Christ. But that seems only to make more wonderful and precious those treasures of truth and joy in Christ which God has ready for those who seek them. They are the more wonderful because one knows that, in the silence which has fallen on many loud voices amid the thunderous cataclysm of war, the Word of God in Christ alone rings out anew. It is the truth of God in Him for this mysteriously muddled and cruel world, and yet the truth which includes every partial element of truth or goodness in the world. And there are such elements. Only second to the wonder of the Gospel of the Cross are the achievements of the souls of very ordinary men under unparalleled afflictions. Without knowing it, they are seen to be worthy of Jesus, Who loves them and gave Himself for them. If there are nearly virgin resources in God, there are also deep unused treasures of potentiality in men. There are in them excellences and simple heroisms which make plain that Christianity is no artificial thing superimposed on human nature, but is the laying bare and setting free of its inmost native quality. There is everywhere about, over here, a diffused Christianity in men who are better than they know. It seems like so much material that needs but a spark to set it ablaze. May there be a great conflagration—the flaming out of the Light of the world, to illuminate, to cleanse, to fill it with the heat of love, both human and divine! AMEN.

THE END

Milton Keynes UK
Ingram Content Group UK Ltd.
UKHW031050120324
439302UK00006B/426